SPILLING OPEN

OPEN

the Art of Becoming
YOURSELf.

SABRINA ward HARRison

Ⓥ

Villard
New York

Thank you so very much

Jennifer Rudolph Walsh
Pamela Cannon

Carol Schneider
Sally Marvin
Anne Godoff
Kelle Ruden
Bruce Tracy
Jay Mandel

Helena Simon

Kathryn Stanbrough.

Patrick Summar
Simon Frankle

Sigid + Andrea at
The Firehouse Home.

Blue
Lynns Yoga

Write to me
Sabrina W. Harrison
511 Telegraph ave.
PMB # 105
Oakland, CA
94609

come Visit my Website

www. Sabrinawardharrison.com

A Bight of
Biafra   Bata
Principe   SP. Gu
(Port.)
Libreville

Comfortable

Sagittarius
experience
you know t
how the lab
dilation of t
is regarded
can wriggle
because you
resemblance
birth. (This i
trouble is, yo
being 8 centi
visualize your
opening

Rob Brezny

BE Blessed

Remembering My own way

and filling my self deep
FIND WONDER

Look for the dream that keeps coming back.

4

overalls monday tuesday wednesday th

Home2sea

Sometimes I wish I was six

...-Dec. 21): Have you ever
...dbirth firsthand, Sagittarius? If so
...e of the primary ways to gauge
...progressing is to measure the
...rvix. A diameter of 10 centimeters
...e threshold at which the fetus
...of the womb. I bring this up
...have a certain metaphorical
...woman on the verge of giving
...e even for you men.) Only
...still at the equivalent of
...rs dilated. So please
...opening ...

A FOREWORD. BY SARK
BACKWARD. FOURWORD. FOUR WORDS:

THIS IS WHAT IS

SABRINA is A luminous mystery,
A CAROUSEL of FEELINGS, lumps
and Discoveries.

IF you could lie Down with
Her JournAls, you would see Genius.

THAT Genius is in THIS BOOK.

Yes SHE is (YOUNG) THank
GOD ÷ we might get that much
More From/of Her.

WHen I reaD This BOOK, I AM
reminDeD of illuminateD manuscripts,

"Deep tALKinG" From AFriCA, sweet spilling teA and FraGrant BeDSHeets.

Your Soul will AwAKen and you MAY FinD your BeD Flying to rare places At niGHT.

Do it.

Get out of your niGHTGown and lie nAKED in MOONLIGHT.

See through SABrina eyes.

I Assure you of A nourishing voyAGe. THere Are words and pictures Here that Move us to Cry and FloAT simultaneously.

Dive Deep.

Be surprised By this Book and the KinDreD Spirit you will FinD inside.

Be Assured of inventions, journeys, and MeSSAGes.

SHe is SHARinG Her reAL self Here and letting us see inside. I celeBrATe Her Soul and All that it contains.

love, SARK

AutHor/Artist Succulent WILD WOMAN

introduction

THE great American POET WALT WHITMAN
said that there is A time We Must
"WASH the gum FROM OUR eyes and Dress
ourselves FOR tHe DAZZle of the Light."
HE looKED at men and women struggling
with tHeir lives and said,
" Long HAVE you timidly WADED holding
A plank by the SHORe, now I Will you
to Be A bold swimmER, to jump off
into the Midst of the SEA, rise again,
NOD to me, SHOUt! and
laughingly DASH with your HAIR."

1 2 3 4 5 6 7 8 9 10

IM Feeling Rather ⟶ DISHEVELED,
and slightly CROOKED
(I SEEM to BE SEEPING out AT THE EDGES.)
I am Sabrina WARD HARRISON
I am twenty One.

THIS IS
MY BOOK.

I OFTEN FEEL AN OVERWELMING PRESSURE to ⟶
"Have It all together"←
WHAT IS "it"?
I FEEL YOUNG.   I am young

Childrens BOOK author and Artist ⟶ maurice
DESCRIBED his creative process   SENDAK
as A "DESCENt into LimBO"
⟶THIS DESCRIBES my ENTIRE LIFE LATELY

THE MORE I LOOK AROUNd and LISTEN
full ⟶ I REALIZE that I'm not alone.

WE ARE all FACING choices tHAT DEFine us.
NO CHOICE, however messy, IS WITHOUT importance
iN tHE OVERALL PICTURE of our lives.
WE ALL AT OUR OWN AGE have to
CLAIM SOMETHING, even if it's only
our own confusion. I AM in the middle
of growing up and into myself.

THIS BOOK is my
LIFE in Progress. A growing
EXPEDITION tHROUGH the tangled an
unFiLLED in PARts of understanding
MY LIFE, MY TRUTH
and myself.

Home2sea

I WANT to share it

welcome inside.

17
18
19
20
21
22
23
24
25
26
27
28
29

19
20
21
22
23
24
25
26
27
28
29
30

THE BASIC. THE ANGRY. THE SAD. the LOST.
The WONDERING. the small ONE.
The DREAMER. THE BELIEVER.
THE YOUNG. THE BRAVE.
THE WEAK. the STRONG.
THE ALONE. The together.
THE SAFE. the unexpected.
the annoying. the insecure. the waiting.
THE WISHER. THE glowing.
the understANDing. THE SCARED.
THE HOLDING BACK. the Letting GO.
THE TRUE and the QUESTION.
THE ME I KNOW. the me I DON'T.

I have been feeling so BLANK
and full of MUTED tones.
I feel just sort of Beige.
I've been stuck in MUCK.

YESTERDAY I got MY HAIR CUT
so SHORT that WHEN I WENT
to SCHOOL CHRISTOPHER Christopher SAID
I looked like AN ENGLISH SCHOOL BOY.
SO THAT DIDN'T HELP.
my face feels wide
and naked.
(...it just looked so good in the magazine.)

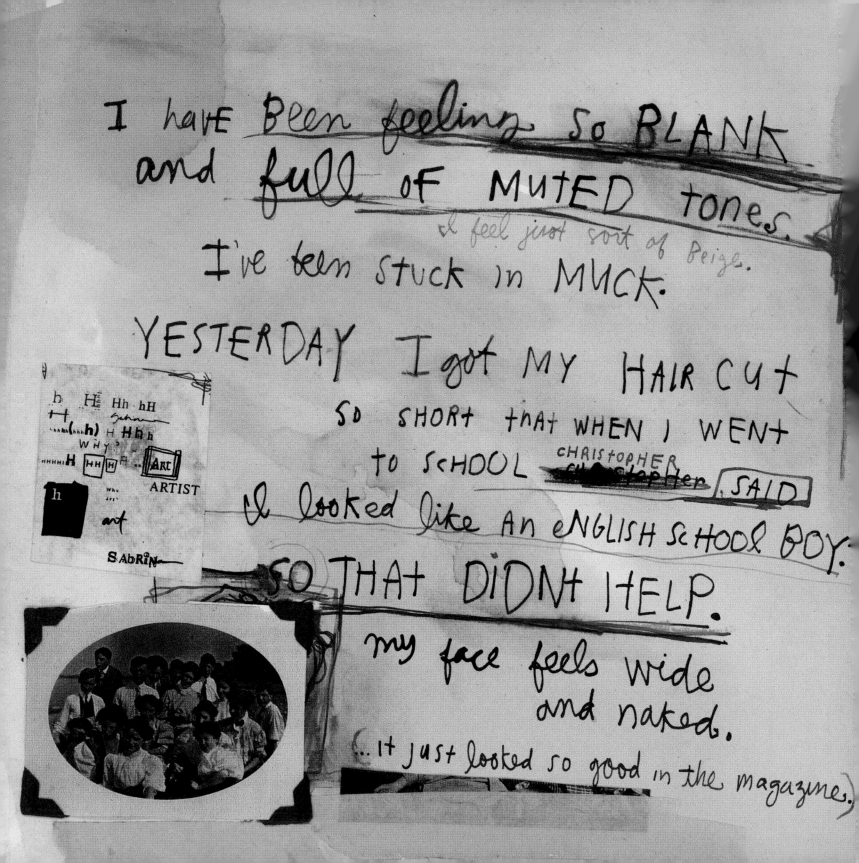

I CATCH Myself trying to COVER up the parts of myself that I dont accept. Its like A MASK.

I USE my Long Black skirts to cover my legs that Feel tHick sometimes

[cover 'up' tight shoes]

I wear my clunky black shoes to GIVE ME SOLID ground and A BIT more HIGHt (I Really trip a lot more though.)

I put MAKE-UP ON that Attempts to look like I DONT have make-up on just to COVER Any SHADOWS OF ACNE.

THIGHS OH...THE WORRIES OF thighs.. thighs thighs.

WHY?

IF I WANT to BE ACCEPTED AND LOVED as is. WithOUT the 'EXtrA Attachments'

why do I keep it up?

this Bewilders me

make up OWN eM.

myo ★ FEAR of what is left 'under it all isnt enough.

4 WHO do I wear a mask FOR today?

I tHInk masks say "ApprovE me"

"ACCEpt ME" "LovE me"

MASKS dont say. → this IS ME as is...

☆ SO WHAT AM I witHout the masks? WHAT am I as I really AM.

FROM the inside OUt? -- 22 %

2

222 I NeveR Passed ALgebRA.

2 I CANt SpEll MucH, I don't really Believe in algebra.

I dont own drawers

I HAD BAD ACNE. I have scars.

IM not SLICK At GAMES involving BALLS, being tHROwN or kicked towards me

I FEEL stumpy

in SWEAtPANtS

(especially ones

witH pockets)

MASKS

2 long skirts

3

So much of my growing up has been spent trying to figure out WHO I am and ~~accept~~

accept WHO I am

and perhaps even love who I AM.

BODY.

unfortunatly I have noticed that I SPEND A LOT of time comparing myself to other young WOMEN my AGE, WATCHING For traits they possess that I feel I lack

It's very EXHAUSTING.

BETTER

THE SHIRT AROUND THE WAIST trick...

★ awkward (REAL) covering up ourselves

dressing up to look casual for a Boy.

"OH to Look "thinner"

1. Long Legs

2. clear skin "RADIANT"

3. thick HAIR

4. THE right "WAKE UP and GO LOOK"

our BODIES make us WORRY.

DON'T QUIT ON YOURSELF.

legs and freckles.

legs

"really get ready"

THE GETTING READY TIME, to look like you didn't really get ready"

★ Deadly INSECURITIES...

E YOURSELF ALL WAYS.

But I seem to keep COMPARING and DESIRING ("NEEDING") MORE or WANTING Less.

WHEN DO I STOP and BE SABRINA the way I am?

when do I stop and believe that I AM ENOUGH as I am?

With all the PARTs of me that feel 'too small' or 'too Lumpy' or 'too Quiet' or not 'edgy' or 'too Deep Feeling' TOO too TOO too.

I must Ask myself "WHAT am I trying to Be that I already AM?"

IF I don't love those parts of me, the tucked in SUCKED in Silent PARTs..

I think it will Be a very SAD journey. and A PATHETIC WASTE of TIME.

"If you're not yourself WHO WILL BE?"

I DON HAVE 10 foot Long Legs.

(and I also CAN'T draw Feet

COVER UP

It's Shocking HOW HARD I AM ON MYSELF. wh..

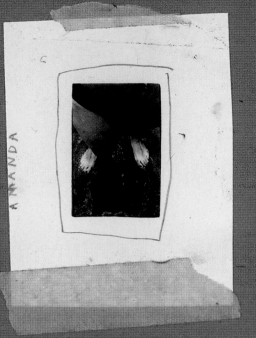

AMANDA

THE truth is WE All ACHE.
WE All HAVE GROWINGPAINS
and WONDER if WE ARE
OKAY and enough + loved.
THE tHInb is — WE ArE.
            REALLy.
WitHout the silver shoes
and lepord print sheets.
WE ARE EnoubH WithOut
all THE thinbs WE Buy,
to make us much MorE
than WE are or need to Be
    WE ARE Simple
      and Complex
        and RArE
            as is.

I struggle with this with my Art + Journal — always wanting to become better+better thinking it will
make me more somehow — Fill the holes that are awkward + unsure. to cover up those parts
with color + pictures. I Hope to become braver at Being bare more + let myoun simple LOVE in
towards myself that loves the fumbling, unsure pieces of me... the saneway the
BOLD daring parts want to GLOW as well → But those part Alone aren't the Answer
And they, certainly are just a small part of me..

LOOKING BACK ON THIS YEAR I can see HOW
I HAVE caused MUCH OF MY OWN SUFFERING
FOR REASONS of PRide, ego and INSECURITY (what is left unsaid)
Pain and ache are felt IN THE unexpressed
PARTS of MY life → WHEN I didn't SPEAK up, spill open
and BE
truely WHO
I AM.

22

60 89 22

NAME

i learn and re-learn
that Silence
DOesn't PrOtEct ME
an unexpressed life is very PAINful to
myself and THOse I LOVE.

DON't LOVE HALFWAY

i am LEARNING
that loving
all the way
can ache + sting, but loving HALFWAY

LOVED

doest keep me SAFE it leaves
ME WITH SADness and
A HOPE
that couLD never
LIVE OUT LOUD. ★

With my freckles
and messy HAIR,
Brused knee
AND chapped Lips —
tHis morning
I AM splendidly
Imperfect and alive.
another BATH it
will Be.

SONA
Op.3

★freckles

MOM and I were WALKING on the BEACh and I WAS explaining to her HOW I wanted to "GET OVER all my INSECURITIES" and "La La..La"... and she looked at me and said "SABRINA, does anyone really feel good about THEMSELVES for MORE THAN 5 Minutes?"

We Both laughed. I was relieved to know she felt that way because she seems SO Graceful, Calm and Beautiful, which she is.. but also full of so much more. Questions, doubts + WONDER. I think that if we can aim for just five minutes a day of complete Acceptance of ourselves, we are doing very well!

M.O.M.

BELONG to yourself.

"HOW one lives as a PRIVATE PERSON is INTIMATELY bound INTO THE WORK. At some POINT I Believe ONE HAS TO stop HOLDING back For FEAR of Alienating some IMAGINARY READER or real ~~read~~ RELATIVE or FRIEND, and COME OUT with personal TRUTH. If we ARE to understand THE Human condition, and if we are to accept OURSELVES in all the complexity, Self DOUBT, extravagance of feeling GUILT JOY the slow Freeing of the self to its full capacity For Action and creation BOTH as Human Being and AS Artist, WE HAVE to know ALL WE CAN ABOUT each OTHER and we have to Be willing to GO NAKED." MAY SARTON.

"WORK Like you _{1 2 3} DON'T need THE money

Love LOVE like YOU'VE NEVER Been HURt

DANCE like no ONE IS WATCHING

— Kathy Mattea

Today was just one of THOSE DAYS
I woke up wanting to go to Italy by car.
perhaps if I really drove fast enough I might
CATCH AIR to FLORENCE
instead of Typography class this morning

Sometimes I forget about the magic.
like the moon and red leaves and HOW
the apples grow AGAIN and AGAIN
Outside my windows.
Life HAS felt overwelming lately

Today in class I had to climb
under the desks during the ~~critique~~ critique
to GET a grip of my "meish-ness" (thats what megan
to find myself again... I don't calls being all yourself)
think anyone noticed me DISAPPEAR.
I can feel so suffocated at School —
WATCHING + THINKING + WONDERING
~~how~~ I fit-in the world...
HOW it can look so easy. "JUST RELAX"

1
2
3
4
5
6
7
8
9
10
11
12
13
14
15
16
17
18
19
20
21

30

MARIANA
BASIN
EAST CAROLINE
BASIN

WOULD I be relaxed
  IN ITALY, spinning under deep night skies?
perhaps... BUT NOW I AM here,
          in BERKELEY California.
I WANT TO GROW COMFORTABLE
with myself HERE NOW.

          so I took off my black skirt
    and big clunky SHOES
I put on overalls and got a slurpie FrOm
    7-11 - turned on TRACY CHAPMAN
  WASHED the makeup off my face,
  And became the ME that I love
  and know the
              BEST.

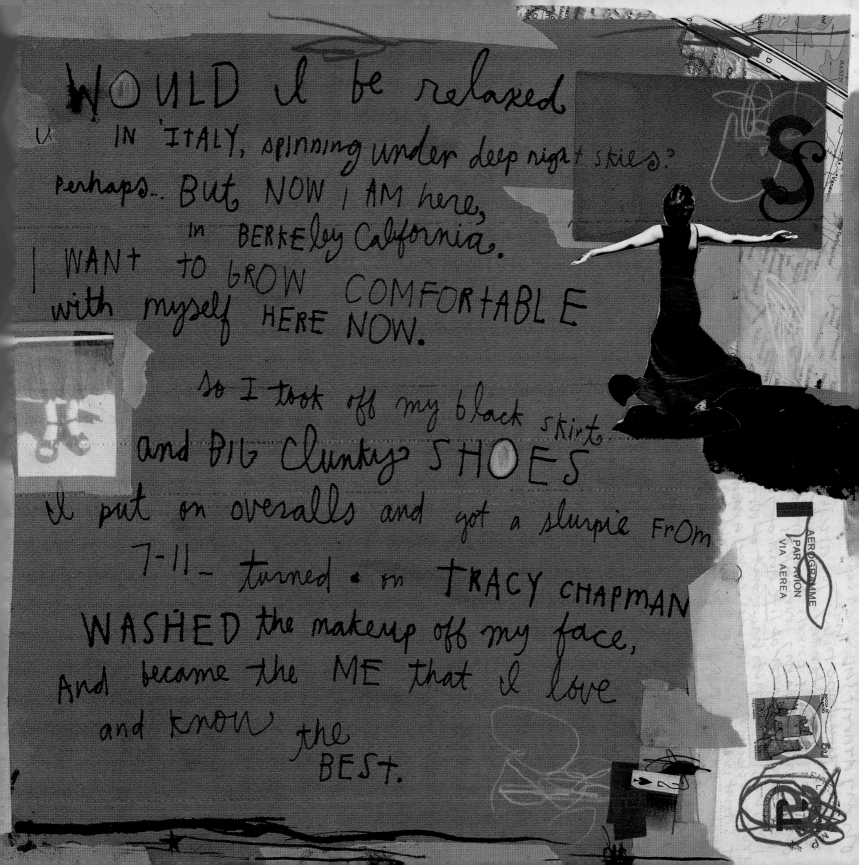

" I certainly DO NOt HOPe to ALTER the world. PerHAPS I CAN PUt IT BEST by saying I HOPE to alter MY OWN VISION Of tHE WORLD I WANt TO ⟶ BE MORE and MORE AS RIDICULOUS as tHAt may SOUNd. "

— HENRY MilleR

14 15 16 17 18 19 20 21 22 23 24 25 26 27 28 29 30

AnD
SUddENLY

it Became
SO
LiGHT

and ClEAR

TÖ the inside..
the HEAViness of
ALL this lifted
and I could
BREATHE into
ME AS I AM

SPRING

MY FRIEND SUSAN ALWAYS reminds
ME THAT THE ULTIMATE GOAL IS
RADICAL SELF ACCEPTANCE.
get into who you are.

THAT IS WHAT INSPIRED ME SO MUCH
ABOUT MEETINg the PHOTOGRAPHER,
ELIZABETH SUNDAY. SHE SAID:

"I BELIEVE in myself. I BELIEVE
IN MY VISION, my life, MY TALENT,
my ART. MORE THAN anyone.
NO ONE CAN TAKE THAT AWAY
FROM ME..."
i THINK when i can get to
THAT place of self acceptance
AND A sence OF CALM assurance

IN WHO I GENUINELY AM - If I CAN
BElieve in WHO I AM, WHAT I
NEED, WHAT I deserve
AND what I MUST
EXPRESS
then I can
Let GO of the struggle
of self acceptance BASED ON
'THEIR' approval of my beauty,
BOOBS, tHIGHS,
or SKETCHBOOKS
I WILL DARE to do just WHAT I do.
Be Just WHAT I AM
and dance WHENever I want
TO

EVERY girl is a princess,
that's a fact. No matter
how **slender**, pretty,
smart, popular **or nice**.
they are all Royalty, a princess in themselfs. If they
believe, they **can** be a pri-

ncess if they look into their
heart and if they think
they are too poor, too u-
gly or not smart, **they**
are WRONG.
TO: Sabrina **FROM!** Meagam

overwhelmed with aching...

WORRY

GIVE

growing

S

GROWING

BARE.

NEED
Wants

MAKE your way   Let go   "THERE ARE places in the heart tha-
NOT yet exist. PAIN MUST BE IN ORDER
tHAt tHEy BE."
— Leon Bloy

I CUT MY HAIR really SHORT. AS the HAIR Fell, I thought

LONGING · TRUTH · THINKING · WONDER · BLA

it as TIME bone by. proof of time passed + growing

K. BALANCE   MUCK   UNSPEAKABLES

LenORD COHEN is playing. I am HOLDING
MY TEARS BacK WITH MY TEETH. THIS MORNiNg
WAS the FIRST Day Of NEEDING my HEATER ON.

we BROKE up.

all tHIS Happened before 4 pm.

7:30 let go of Alex my love
9 am chokeD on tEA
10:25 got lockeD out
and HAD to CLIMB through
A TINY WINDOW
with spider WEBS
2:45 FELL
HARD, while
running to Buy
FILM for CAMERA
3:00 SCRAPED
  a. kneE
  b. elBOW
  c. SHOULDER
  d. EAR
3:00 TAUGHT TWO
ART and Discovery
classes FOR the first tIME

empty SPACE

so I guess IF I could make it
THROUGH tHAT it WIll BE
OKAY

that feeling of absolute
naked running
Euphoria

unfillable
3 year old

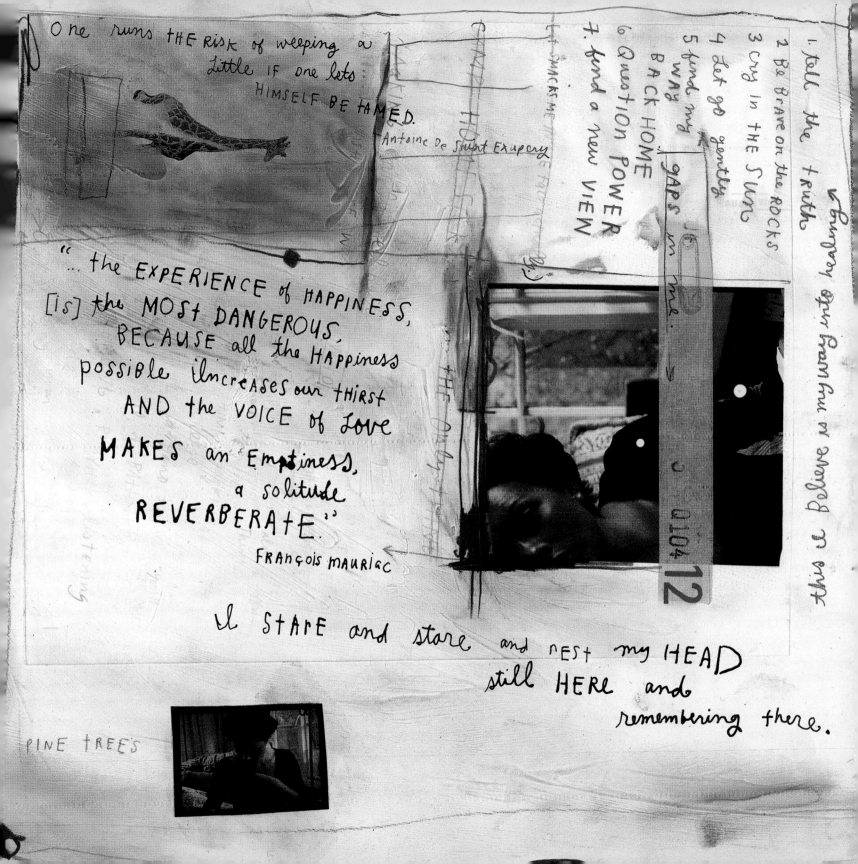

One runs THE RISK of weeping a
little if one lets
HIMSELF BE TAMED.

— Antoine De Saint Exupery

1. tell the truth
2. Be Brave on the ROCKS
3. cry in THE SUN
4. let go gently
5. find my way BACK HOME
6. Question POWER
7. find a new VIEW

"... the EXPERIENCE of HAPPINESS,
[is] the MOST DANGEROUS,
BECAUSE all the HAPPiness
possible ilncreases our thirst
AND the VOICE of Love
MAKES an Emptiness,
a solitude
REVERBERATE."

FRANÇOIS MAURIAC

I STARE and stare and rest my HEAD
still HERE and
remembering there.

PINE TREES

LOSS AND LETTING GO OF MY ACHE
It CAN FEEL so dumb and
POINTLESS and so sad and real
OTHER times.

I Feel 1. shaky
2 RED
3 WORRIED
4 sore head
FALL DOWN 5 spinning eyes
6 sick WITH DOUBT
7. exhausted

AFTER

I dont like how afraid MY
HANDS are to BE empty

1 no ATTENTION TO BOUNDARIES.

POMPADO
TEEKANNE
AUS DEM HAUSE TEEKANNE

POMPADOU
TEEKANNE
AUS DEM HAUSE TEEKANNE
POMPADOUR TEE-HANDELSGES. MBH.
GERMANY
2,25g N

I CAME HOME TODAY FROM SCHOOL VENTING
VERY LOUDLY IN THE CAR TO MYSELF. STAGES
I FEEL SO "HIGHLY SENSITIVE" and OF
SPUNOUT and TIRED and HOPELESS LIGHT
AND THAT FEELS SCARY! I AM TIRED
OF THIS DRAMA WITH THIS BOY AT SCHOOL.
I WANT SINCERITY and I WANT BRAVE LOVING
I dont WANT to BE MAKING
a LOGO OR DESIGNING an Annual REPORT

I WANT TO MAKE BOOKS
AND TAKE Pictures and drink more tea
AND LIE on more couches
and Listen to PABLO NERUDA poetry
and READ SARK BOOKS
AND GO TO BED early
and KISS MORE cheeks AND
play HEADS·up·7up when It RAINS
and giggle MORE and DRIVE LESS
AND Dream up Funny POSSIbilities
AND BRAVE ENDINGS.

1

2

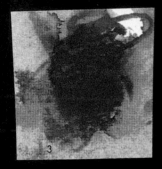

3

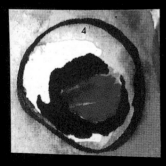

4

5

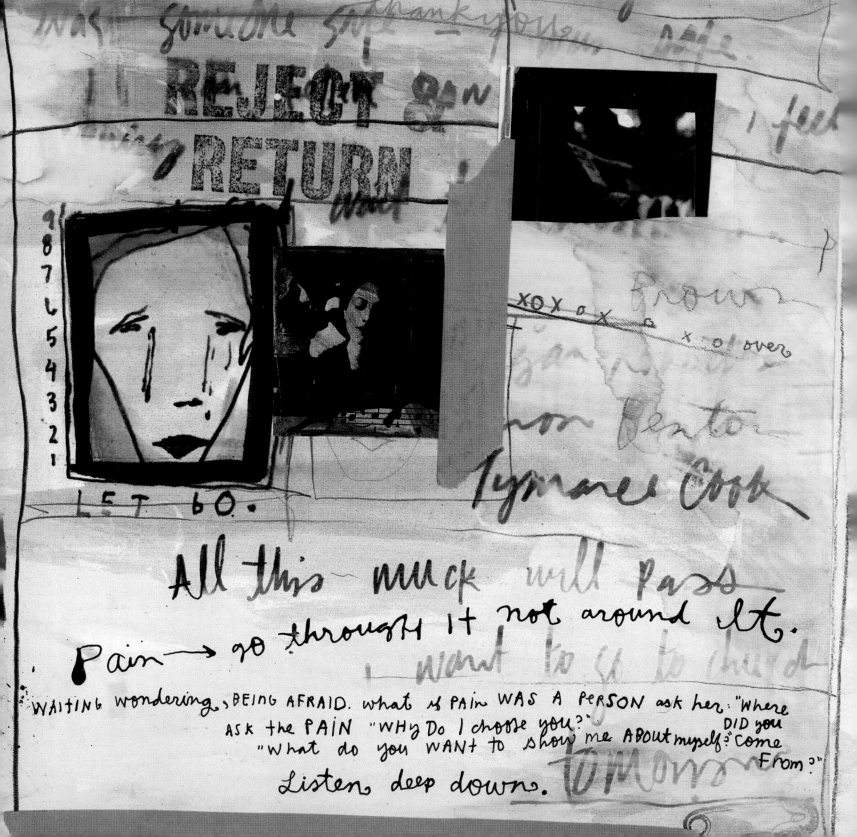

REJECT &
RETURN

9
8
7
6
5
4
3
2
1

LET GO.

XO XO X O X O over

Tymaree Cook

All this muck will pass

Pain → go through it not around it.

WAITING wondering, BEING AFRAID. what if PAIN WAS A PERSON ask her "Where
ASK the PAIN "WHY Do I choose you?"   DID you
"What do you WANT to show me ABOUt myself?" Come
                                                                                    From?"
Listen deep down. Tomorrow

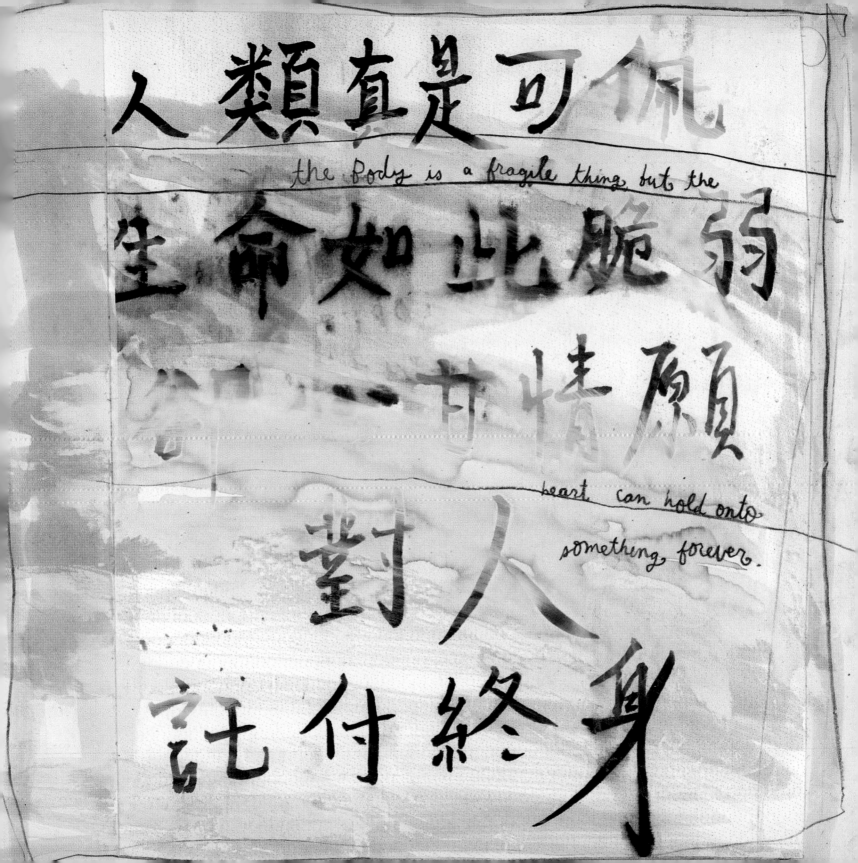

A STORM HIt YESTERDAY
the moon was so bright
that It wouldn't let me sleep.
the Day HAS Felt invisible
like time couldn't
make ITSELF known

I WANT TO TWISt

away from this

Loneliness,

there seems to be
NO PLACE
for it in
this world
around me.

Where DOES
everybody else put tHEIR
Sadness.

I FEEL SAD On the inside, if not shown.

Praying

so who am I in this crumbled rawness?

I feel like swiss cheese ⟶
what goes in the lonely holes?
new light?
FRESH AIR?

I'VE been NOTICING tHE ROOts PuSHINg up tHROuGH the SIDEWALK.

Im trying to REMEMBER my Root LoVE IN my LIFE, FROM thoSE WHO know me deeply.
home
1. mom
2. dad
3. Anna
4 NANA
5 megan Brian AARON ★

'Loss made everything Sharp'. -May Sarton

Driving to class with him, All I could think about WAS tHAT it HAD been three days since I'd touched his FACE... AND HE SEEMED so fine.

I SAID, ~~you~~ → "you seem like you
to HIM, DIDN'T miss
a BeAt!"

He looked at me
and said
"SAbrina, I've missed
so many BeAts, I've
MADE A RhytHM."

DO I know more now?
¹ My Questions
² MY INTUITION
³ my blushing HOPE
⁴ My ACHE
were All A PArt OF the
EXPERIENCE
of Falling in LOVE
and IF I DID it OVER
ild Feel It All again—
hopefully WORRY LEss and
Surrender MORE.

CANt Being Just AS I Am be enough FOR Me?

I dont Like doubting my 'ME-ish-ness'
because its ALL I HAVE
ANd I dont have time to keep
SeARching to Be someone else.

HIP GIRL

I WANt the Wide HUBS And the exclamations of delight.

WHEn did I StARt DOUBting WHO I AM?

my FRiend MARguerite who is tEN just cant comprehend not Being Herself.

Thats Why she is SO VIBRANtly Alive and glorious.

study to know yourself as you really are
I think WE HAVE A HARD tiME MAKing A commitment WHEN
We dont KNOW WHO WE ARE. So who am I?
It seems to Be EASIER to think of WHO Im not.
★ Im not MAdonnA OR SUPERMAN.

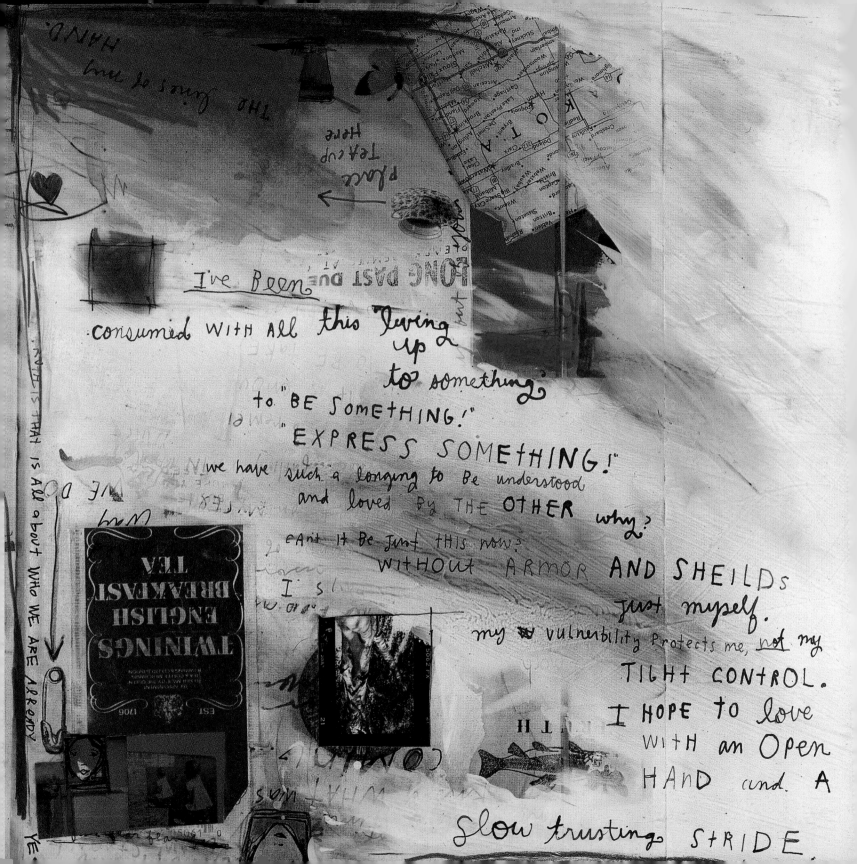

The lines of my HAND

place Teacup Here

LONG PAST DUE

I've Been

consumed WITH ALL this "living up to something"

to "BE SOMETHING!"

"EXPRESS SOMETHING!"

we have such a longing to Be understood and loved By THE OTHER why?

cAnt it Be Just this now? WitHOUt ARMOR AND SHEILDS Just myself.

my vulnerability Protects me, not my TIGHt CONtROL.

I HOPE to love WitH an Open HAnd and. A

slow trusting StRiDE.

WHO IS THAT IS ALL about WHO WE ARE ALREADY. YE.

TWININGS ENGLISH BREAKFAST TEA EST 1706

I am
In the NEW little NOOK I have made
In my kitchen.
(an upside down wheel as a
running and tea table)
I have made PANCAKES and IRISH CREAM coffee
...A COMPLETE "JUST ADD WATER BreakfAST"
I HAVE WOKEN UP with ache and a quiet empty feeling.
I CAN HeAR BOB Dylan *IN the Backround
singing 'I Want you so BAD'
I feel quite lost INSIDE myself,
as if tHeY would just
APPEAR and solVE tHE GROWing
Questions I seem to
like im looking for my train tracks
FOR my LIFE.
(★ Be Blessed)
Questions
I seem to FACE
as I meet   my self
my
reflection iN
the morning.

Perhaps we write tWARDS
BECOME from

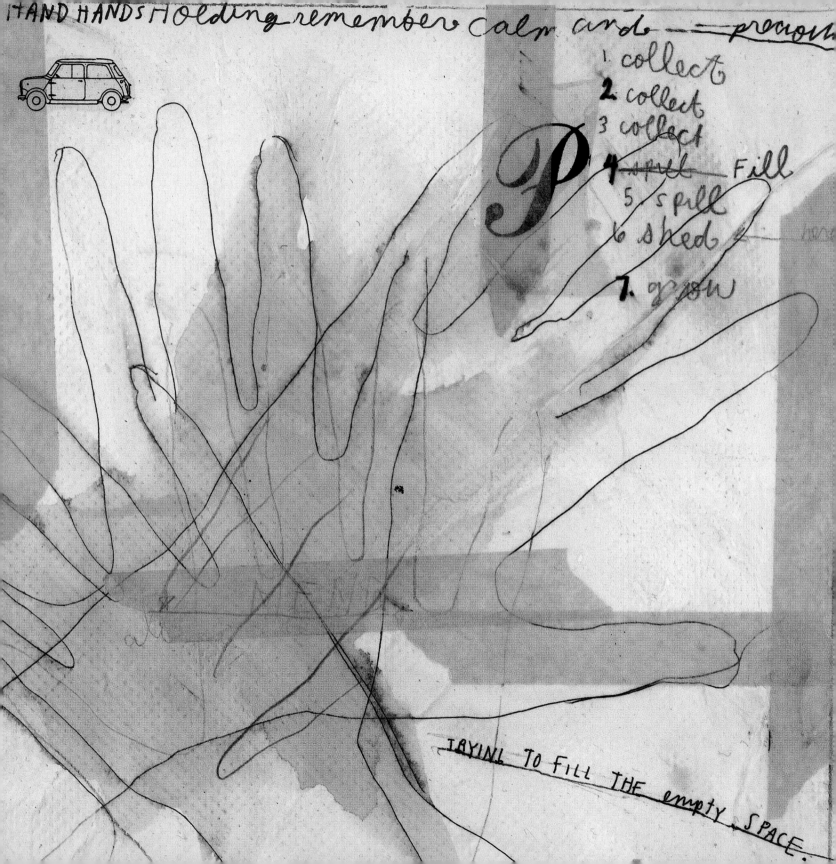

HAND HANDS Holding remember calm and ——— precious

1. collect
2. collect
3. collect
4. ~~spill~~ Fill
5. spill
6. shed
7. grow

𝒫

TRYING TO FILL THE empty SPACE.

I don't know
   if I will
ever understand
 this Ache.
   perhaps It is
Simply + completely
   Love and

   what

   HAPPENS.
       at the end.

"   ~~Loss~~ LOSS

CANT FIT

NOVEMBER 17, early Morning

I am HERE NOW I'm not there anymore.
with Him.
Life is carrying ON and I flash with
A MIXTURE of PANIC and faith at the truth
of this. LIFE will keep GOING.

A.L GREEN is playing TIME just slips AWAY
I AM thinking ABOUT HOW MUCH I try to cling to ~~balance~~
BALANCE. and the fact is—
It's not gonna feel BALANCED for a WHILE!
is REAL Living, "BALANCED" ANYWAY?

I CAN't control WHEN I HEAL, BUt I CAN WATCH
WHAT HAPPENS, and try to BE EVER·SO·GENtLE with thE ACHE
WHEN im sitting
WHEN It COMES tO ME on my Floor IN A Slip
AND tEARS stuck too far down.

I FEEl a SURGE in me to Love,
and IT CAN'T BE REACHED.
I FEEL NUMB.

THERE IS A REASON
and there is A
MEANING.. you will
KNOW IN time,
BUT   time itself
         will
            choose
   the moment.
   —KENt NeRBurn

I TALKED to NANA this morning. SHE HAS SUCH GOOD
things TO SAY ABOUt living.
      She SAID I SHOULD tAKE CARE of the PAIN
I'm feeling. the SAME WAY I should take caRE of
the scRap on MY knee (from my Fall last week.)
SHE SAID GIVE it AIR AND SUN
      DON't PICK At IT
            Let it HEAl.
So I shall inrimitate my knee.
   THE SCAR ON MY knee will BECOME PaRt of
   A memory of the feelings of Falling on THE Ground —   MY StorY.
                              AND FALLING IN LOVE.

I've been home for a set of family and caring,
and now my COURAGE today is to fly home to Berkeley
even WHEN IT FEELS SO COMPLICATED
confusing and
Lonely sometimes.

"MOST OF LIFE IS JUST ABOUT SHOWING UP."
-WOODY ALLEN

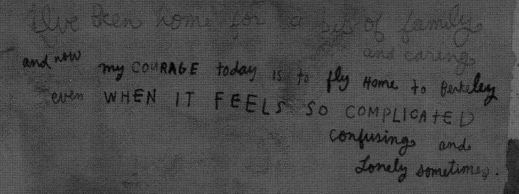

stuff to think about and go back to Berkeley:
1. Read
2. Hills
3. THANKSGIVING at Amandas
4 changing room
Breathe
beach body
During Dancing turning 22.

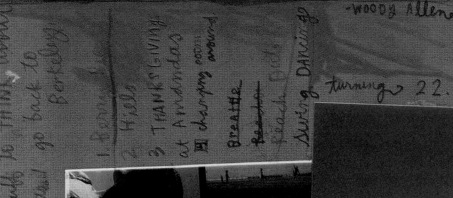

RB 200 KODAK   3 A 200

making YOUR Life. FEEL better,

1 I think it TAKES A BIT of A LOT of things.
+ let the tears roll where they will.

2 money on ANYTHING. SARK in Anyshape.

3 a VERY SOFT OLD HAND saying "you'll Be OKAY."

4 AN INVITATION to A BATHTUB

or stretching ————————→ praying

6 Listening to Children explain.

7. WATching the BrAnches let GO.

8

9 sharing your colors.

forgive me

love wings

P

1939

these are the days that must happen to you.
WHITMAN

So when I just feel the loss
and the sadness — I think,
Why love if it HURTS THIS MUCH

I try, just a Bit to SOAK IN the goodness
OF FEELING

So deeply, FOR
ANOTHER — the
SURRENDER,
the joy, and
the TANGLED
Laughter
is also
IN the
PAIN
FELT.

this was the first flight

slow

I will ALWAYS HOLD THIS PLACE

the C.S. Lewis love story

ieve

all Sabrina and

in a Frame

may 17th

"The Pain now is a
Part of the happiness
then, that's the deal."
SHADOWLANDS.

Let yourself go.

~~from~~

SHIFt

i just ~~had~~ had a brainstorm of fun
things to do! hooray for ~~Sab~~ ♥
• paint your nails w/ glitter nail polish
  (i have glitter polish on my nails)
• eat Welch's lemonade popsicles
• buy pillsbury sugar cookie dough & snack heartily
• daydream about dashing
  men, italian gardens, long
  moonlit walks
  dont smile like that!
remember: everything is
as it should be (seize the
uncertainty!) rest + relover FULLY before jumping
back into it-better to be ~~████~~ fully Sabrina again...
rather than still-sick-sleepy-amy Sabrina. You are
magical! have my strength

BOSTON COLLEGE
Founded 1863
POST CARD
photo by ...

USA 20c
H.S.Truman

Sabrina!
509
La

M ♥

From Megan →

Begin here.

I don't want to
edit my Living,
my Becoming WHO I AM.

its like trying to fit into shoes that arn't mine   ballet slippers +
        ~~just~~   knotted RIBBONS.

I've Been FEELing Blocked and FAR TOO ALONE inside.
All this Holding Back ————→ clutchingon
All the Silent Thinking "Will he 's disappear?" "How long will it last?"
                                        "Is this RIGHt?"
Maybe Im just such a Romantic, ~~still~~ wanting treasured moments
    Dreams and plans + Visions of Trips into the redwoods
~~Pic~~ Picnics on my Floor with Paint on our Fingers → Kisses
        FAR too much teA and reading outloud.
   sss   •••••

I just don't want the time to be spent ~~for~~ wondering if it would be "TOO MUCH" to call and check-in and have a little ~~s~~ sweet Time

Lying ~~—~~ under the Oak Trees At Craigmont Park

Nicola said to me this wonderful thing

"I Believe that Loving Fearlessly is the Bravest thing in this world.

Its ~~not~~ loving without Fear.

Its Loving FEAR-LESS-ly, couragously

LOVE Truly

to Be ~~af~~ afraid and leap regardless....

There is Such POWer in that."

Let yourself go

I think that realates to all parts of living your life.

I think what is left un-lived + unexpressed in Love, Hurts the most.

NORTH BEACH PIZZA — a tuesday in November with Ale,
WE ATE pizza in dim red light
WE WANTED Answers and ~~each other~~
speaking into THE HARD PARTS to ~~say~~.   EACH OTHERS HANDS.

IT SEEMED to be
Raining questions
and ache.

all this Fear of Love ~~leaving your colors and~~
• my ART + Discovery
class. ARiel says "I'm AFRAID of nothing."
then Lilli and Katie respond the SAME.   I gave Him THE LITTLE PRINCE
makes me think of the children in
FIVE yearolds are ~~FEARL~~
FEARLESS.

(some of)
My 21 yearold FEARS
1. dark streets
2. The BACK of my Thighs.
3. Being Laughed at
4. Being FOllowED
5. Being A Wimp.
6. 'JUST Being Lucky'
7. the rain not stopping
8. NOT Having anything to Give.
9. GOSSip
10. Perms
11. JR. High
12 ACNE
13 earthquakes on Bridges
14. Falling in Love
15 LOVE Quitting On me
16. Dying → worse, not really living!

Fix it kit

the ~~~~ NEXT class of ~~~~ nine year olds
understand WARS and buns,
BEing LEFT all alone + Forgotten
the FEAR is growing
in the DARK.

BUT IT keeps GOING, AND GOING: GOOD.

sometimes it
feels so hard.
Love   to be Brave on THE ROCKS

FEAR
1 Recieving
2 Replacing
3 Rethinking
4 Remembering
5 Regreting
6 Rejecting

It's amazing what happens when I release
the grip.

LOVE love   love today

1. Honey on crackers.

Intimacy.
2. My dads voice
reading a story

9. Unseen Laughter

delight

a diet Coke and a walk around the corner.
DOOR CLOSING
★ releasing the "whats next" worry. 6. Spilling Kisses
7 ADMitting LOVE.
• Bare feet • long grass.   +TEACH ME
                                                    Not Feeling guilty.   LOVE.
singing loud.   8. releasing the grip.
TOASTED BAGLES

Natalie Merchant
Rosemary Boquets   10. singing anything.

strength.

GUILTY Stove. I DON'T know   love is.
got TIRED from the FIGURING IT ALL OUT

Before my 22nd Birthday, I would wish to commit to grow younger to let go of my fear as I LEARN About Love. to allow All to be felt

secret answers

THERE IS STILL SO MUCH Newness AND wonder to Feel

unfold

BELIEVE

Bless tHE NOT KNOWN

★ telling my truth in Love is like exposing the underside of my wings

I think about

His grin lines

HOW

it really feels.

HIS FINGERS SLIPPED IN MINE

the

Only SHOULDERS

way to grow only Human connection

is

that TRUTH.

WE SEE THAT PART only when we fly.

[DARE]

I thought a lot today about Limitless Love.
Most of the time I spend worrying
About the people in my life who
love me conditionally — WITH LIMITS

deciding WHEN and HOW
they will love me and
HOW they will Edit the
love they will
Show me.

The Problem lies in how I then
Edit and Limit the LOVE
I am showing and giving
(for fear of not being loved in return)
And thats not how I want
to live in Love.

ACCORD

I Sat on THE BENCH outside of class today,
and talkED to Jon.
I READ to Him From my Journal,
it WAS the PART ABOUt the ACCORDIAN player I
WAS WATCHing on the street last weekend.

HE SAID that an accordian is such
A Perfect metaphor for Love,
Because you are ~~the~~
Always opening,
AND closing, shifting,
And getting AIR,

I SAW MY
REflectION
in the
Window
and saw
something
Diffrent in
MY EYE

AND
thats
HOW
the
music
happens.

true.

THEY

the Parked
windows —

where was
she at
verify OnE?

Something HARD
to Describe

Muted and Tired
and rather
concerned

☆ IF Rebecca WAS HERE I would
tell her that the pink Jasmine is blooming
Again.
I WOULD tell HER THAT I
Felt AFRAID to Ride my bike
HOME FRom DANiels House
Last Night & ~~dont~~ didnt tell
                                    him.
I WANTED to Be embrACED
And smooched + tickled and
WONderfully whispered to
By Him but I WASnt.
        I HELd BACK
        I couldnt Relax

missing Rebecca downstairs

TIME boo bA? ~~Boo bA reeyover~~ wow? dweller

seeing

At home

It WAS tHAt kind of holding back
tHAt I dont even know WHAt I'm
WITHOLDing—And I just ~~don~~
Didn't know why I Felt so crumbly

1 2 3
   4 5
6 7 8

all in here

I Pretended to Be asleep
so I wouldnt HAVe to
deal with that awkward silence.

silence

IM just Not sure
what is Going on inside
me.

what Answers AM I
suppose to be arriving At?

Why AM I heRE

And
Not tHEre?

I HATE WAITING FOR A BOY to ARRIVE! (OR call)

so I won't, I'll write. won't

I'm trying to not think ABOUT it →

But its so Annoying when they dont keep their WORD!

The thing that Ive been noticing About myself is that I dont make it clear what is important to me — Because I dont want to lose the connection or seem like I'm too much WORK to them.

But then I Become too much WORK FOR myself because I'm not being True to myself.

swim

It isnt my job to judge what is "TOO MUCH" For them.

My JOB is to Be compleatly HOnest and myself and And let the other person respond honestly. With who They are and what feels right to them.

I must not shift, ALTER or HIDE myself IN ORDER to Experience LOVE — because thats when thats not really Love — thats when resentment is BORN.

I catch myself trying to Be cool + dont care.

OH

Spinning   SUN   Hard.

I need

and secret things

I NEED myself.

I NEED

GENUiness   I need

true. Loving gestures   lots

IN

HALfWay

to Surrender

not Be MOCKED

I need True kindness

BRightly

this weekend HAS felt so out of control

LOts of FEARS

★ Not Good at Loving

Im Not GOOD looking.

im NOT GOOD At Making stuff Happen.

Im NOt GOOD At ARTiCULATing HOW I FeeL.

...Not good at spelling

.. Not good at tating care of what I love.

→ And with all these ~~fears~~ Feelings comes Hopelessness

I feel like IM drowning IN ~~the~~ feeling sorry for ~~myself~~

trying to
MEAsure up

I Feel PAthetic + tired of Being me.

AMOUNTS FORWARDED

NET AMOUNT DAY RECEIVED

RECEIVED FROM RECEIVED

GENERAL ACCT.

REQ. U. S. PAT. OFF. STANDARD CASH RECEIVED RECC

No 61 19 MONTH OF RECORD OF CASH RECEIVED

sitting in THE CAR WITH Alex IN THE Middle oF trying to get out OF THE DARK tHICK feelings, I said "I guess it WILL Be okay" AND HE SAID "YES, but Its okay Now too."

THIS reAlly confused me because all day I Was trying to "GET OVER IT." FORGET my feelings HIDE My FEELings from HIM + From myself I slowly began to see how right he was.

Its okay NOW

these feelings ArE NORMAL and have to be allowed to BE Felt and seen.

WE HAVE TO TRUSt tHAT OUR FRIENDs WONt Quit on us WHEN we Are HOpeless — and even more — WE Can't Quit on Our own selves

WE ArE all WE HAVE deep down — and all we can save.

as I am

Ideal
Ideal
IDEAL
IDEAL
vision
of perfect coverage

*. I WANT to show
THE P.J.s before
THE BALL GOWN. WHY do I WANT
to SHOW my BASIC self. (AS IF ITS SOME SHAMEFUL reality)
ISN't It MORE SHAMEFUL
loving just AS I AM.

CINCO DE MAYO
USA 32

HIDE HIDE

I WANT to stop sucking IN
$TOP Holding My Breath
STOP COVERING up.

Let go. → It isnt worth it.
I cant tHINK OF ONE GOOD Reason
to keep up tHE Act of 'Being MORE than I need
(or Less)
IF I CANT LOVE myself BARE + Freckled,
THEN 'HE' certainly cant love me.

trying to change myself to fit some Ideal'
SEEMS to Be An endless + DEHYDRATING
WAY to live

VOICE of

" Im AFRAID to Show
YOU WHO I really AM,
Because if I SHOW YOU WHO
I really AM, you might
not like it
and thats all ive got. "

stop

ALL tHe PARTS

HIDE Your real Self!

IF WE LET (lets)
OURselves
Be truly SEEN,
tHAN WE CAN BE
TRuly LOVED. SARK.

+ HIDE
YOUR
FECKles.
CE HOARD
ACE WitHOut
Freckles is like
Sky WitHOut
Stars."

WHEN I WAS 11 I
WAS told by A
Friend in the neighborhood
that A mixture OF Lemon
Juice
and cottage cheese
would take off my Freckles...
I remember putting it all
over my Arms
and WAiting.

E is just too short.

stop

I WAS HATED
myself
For
my
Freckles
and thinking it
would actually work!
just WASN't A Blonde tAN BABE.
And still Am Not.

★ sometimes I feel like IM
in A very unloved BODY.

Be + HIDing wHat I AM.

dont Quit on myself.
Its All IVE GOt.

WISH

NOT so sensitive

ONE PART
OF ME
feels
so tired
of trying
to feel
Okay
with
myself

HIDING BEHIND MYSELF

SOMETIMES I feel

very very ins

feelin'
thick

FROM THE INSIDE

MORE is never enough.

my neck gets so red
WHEN I'M
nervous

THE PART Just
WAnts the phone
to ring

Big heart
in here. open
full.

SHAKING   As wide as I can

DISTRACTIONS
TAKE ME
AWAY FROM the inside WORLD
of endless
WOnders +
worries
Im not always
feeling Wonderful

leap   artist!

You are so young

I would beg of you, dear FRIEND, as well as I can you stand Before BEGINNINGS.

to HAVE PATIENCE WITH everything that remains unsolved in your HEART

and to try to love the questions themselves like LOCKED ROOMS and like books written in a very foreign LANGUAGE

I WANT the Love in my Life to FEEL like A deep BREATH, a blushing laugh, A View across the Sea of Cortez ALWAYS EXPANDING and WIDER glowing.

I WANT the experience of love to LIFT ME UP and Dance during dinner, even when my little SISTER says she'll pay me $5.00 not too.

still open.

swing dancing and STAR GAZing.

OR PERHAPS

(Loving in my own WAY.)

Tells How I really Feel inside

I AM LEARNING to reinvent WHAT being WITH A BOY can be like MayBE its A FORT instead of A MOVIE, WITH lots of SHEL SILVERStien READING out loud (tHE Missing Piece meets the Big 'O' is A FAVORite) OR A SPRING night WITH Tea and ART on the floor.

MOSS ROCKS
(or tacos)

acorns,
wheat,
black berrys,
PINE TREES
SHADOWS

AGE
LIFE
TWILIGHT
tank top
MORNING

english
breakfast
TEA
with cream

NIGHT

Feeling
tHE
fabric
of the
moment
(susan talked
about this)

One day this week I found myself looking at
_____ lens lined up on my

whirling
parade of jar.

in LovE

summer.

I got a tiny RED pair of
WOODEN SHOES
that
they

SAND SHADOWS

LAKE DRIBBLES
& ideas

(I must)

Be sure to Be   Be Sir

this, (before looking for it in someone else)
(or expecting)

Today I noticed

WIDE NIGHT SKY

. BELIEVE + SUPPORT → not JOKE + MOCK

· MATING DRAGON FLIES

· Spill OPEN

crackling FIRE... oh the smell...

tAKES MOONLIGHT Explores

OPERA MUSIC Puccini La Bohème

Wide Laughter

Loves DEEPly

tells how it Feels inside

an abandoned DAD

Appreciates decadance in creative ways.

Reading Pablo Neruda in the trees shade

·A LAKE under a pink twilight

A tender + genuine Lover

lOoking like Flickering SAMON

Believing in GOD Forgiveness + wonder

· KitcH CANADA

faith

· Being enough.

noon watching

susan call
up here at
DE Gras
we laughed a
laughed an
spoke gent
about silent
REJECTION
(book)
MEN sho
come for din
On the 21
with mo
DA

LOVE

TiL

thank you mom and Dad

★ the trip became an adventure of sorts.
MOM + DADs anniversary is Today.
20 years of hanging Out together
a goodnight + goodbye
• THE sound of EArly morning coffee + Ideas
first dawn
Reflection On the NAVY lake • HAVing children
whistle of crickets to
garden talking   Laughing, HARD
Crackle Fire
PAD tHai   cooking Wild Dinners
NIGHt HUM
Being Real Deep supporters
Italian dinners
an old pal to   COMPANIONS
notes
• the dock   Pals

                       Lovers
                       PARENtS
                       I wonder if I will ever know
                       this feeling one day?
                       (i really hope so. really. REALLY.)

CANADA

to brass

secret trail

A Weekend
in San Diego with a
dear Brian

my Best boy friend picture Mot
A
Picnic over the Ocean at
                    sundown
with laughter + wide
              conversation

all I could wish for

                perspective

picnic

Brians Friendship
Arrived some summer
afternoon years ago,
With Bare Feet;
        and a grinn

Brian

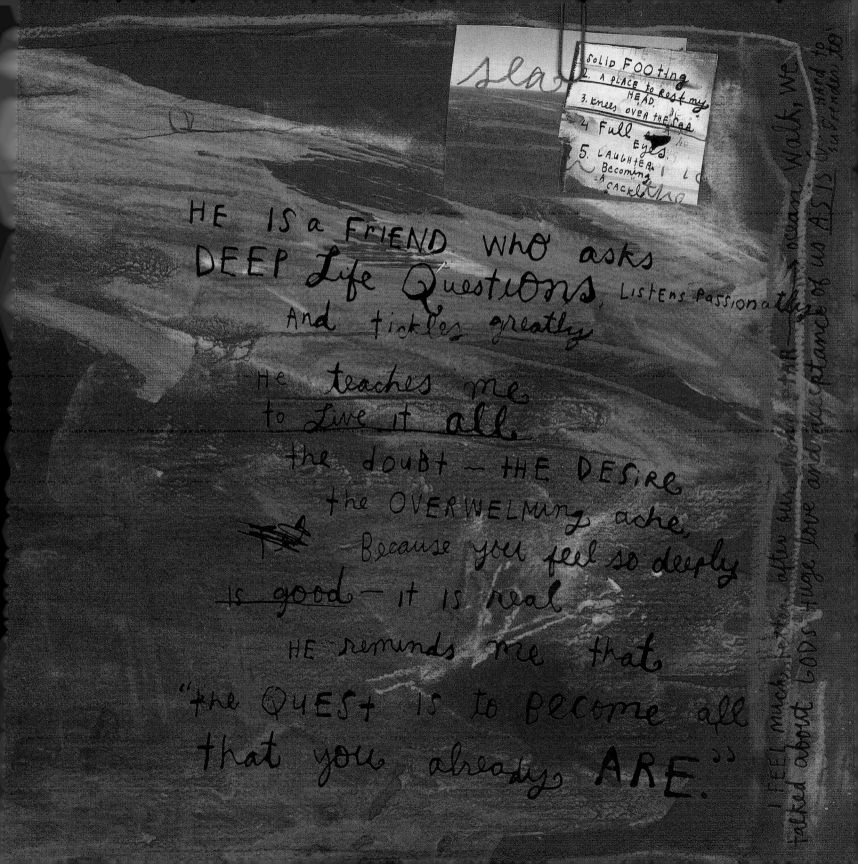

sea

1. SOLID FOOTing
2. A PLACE to REST my HEAD.
3. KNEES OVER THE Sea
4. FULL EYES.
5. LAUGHTER: LO
   Becoming a CACKLE

HE IS a FRIEND WHO asks
DEEP Life Questions, LISTENS Passionately
And tickles greatly

HE teaches me
to Live it all

the doubt — THE DESiRE
the OVERWELMING ache,
Because you feel so deeply
is good — it is real

HE reminds me that
"the QUEST is to BECOME all
that you already ARE."

I FEEL much better after our ocean walk. We talked about GOD'S Huge Love and acceptance of us AS IS. 4 September 10

I WANT to TOUCH ON All THE Sides
OF LOVE — THE HOPE + Gladness
as WELL as THE ANXIETY + Ache.
THE BIGGest thing About Love that
I HAVE DISCOVERED IS tha LOVE isn't
just ONE WAy — there isn't just
A Point of PERFECTion THAT MAKES
it "All okay + GREAT FROM NOW ON."

I am Discovering that what I
am needing to learn in life is gonna
KEEP coming up. Oh yes!
THIS Morning I WOKE up From A VERY restless
sleep with Anxiety about replacement.
And I just exclaimed to myself
HAVEN'T I LEARNED this YET?
haven't I learned HOW to handle these
Feelings yet? the answer: NOPE.

"FOR ONE human being to LOVE another is perhaps the most difficult, the ultimate test. task of all, the epitome It is that striving FOR WHICH ALL OTHER striving is mere merely preparation."
RAINER MARIA RILKE

TRUER

MOM MY AGE

I AM learning to write + speak OF MY tRUe Feelings for myself, thats HOW I CAN Let Go sooner + LOVE Fuller. It's [A] MIXTURE OF speaking up + speaking in... reaching out and REACHING IN.

Pine WOOD. DANGLING BitS of the WORLD.

tHis way.

lemonHONEY Drink
SHORt HAIR + GinGer tEA
ROME

← Alexander 5

pug

OH whAt AM I learning?... sketchbooks smell different from One anotHER.

to Be alive — to Be Okay with all thAt I DON't understAnd still. (driving to SAntA Paula just to get to tHE BOY I wAnt to kiss.)

All tHE "HOW COMEs" and "MayBe I shoulds"

Tonight, Alex and I sAt in A dim Booth sipping cokes, I knew again Why all of tHis—
To grow — more alive.

to experience being alive and being brought alive by another something & so beautiful and rare. it reminds me of that Henry Miller line... "I want to become more + more myself as ridiculous as thAt MAY sound."

in LOVE I Become WHO I must understAnd.

BEGIN

in love

A. laughing
B. PAPER
c. crying
D. listening
E. PHOtos
F. TIME
g. music
H. cArs
I. SEA
J. Books
K. BEDS
L. kissing imissyou

new
VIEW

SKY

I FIND MYSELF

COMPARING a lot — thinking "OH I SHOULD be MoRE like her" "he is less LIKE HIM" La La La.

But when I let go of the world all around me and BREATHE into ME as I AM — I can LOVE much more truly + compleatly ~~+ cope~~

WHEN I can accept myself I can accept the ones around me.

And BE still
together
enough as WE are.

that the real PARt.
(connect)
all tHERE. is.

all THERE IS /

all tHERE is.

REAL IS all there is.

It is now noon 🐝🐝🐝 at ROMA cafe. ⭐

IVE GOT THIS GREAT NEW PEN.
to write with. this afternoon.
AND THAT SEEMS to BE the
only thing, that is getting me
TO WRITE SOMETHING

I HAVE Been coloring-in
Previous BARE PAGES

and drinking + redrinking, my   tea
CUP OF JASMINE tEA.
A. Ive HAD three cups of tea.
B. three PITA BREAd, some hummu
C. and A non-FAt YOGERt ←   hymus

yogert #15 A
HARD WORD to
spell

I HAVE Been WATCHING A
WOMAN A fEW tABLES AWAY
reading ANNE Lamott

also reAD ←   HEr BOOK OPERATING instructions
BIRD
BY   so many expressions
BIRd.   covered her FACE as SHE reads FROM PAGE to PAGE.
THAt BOOK Brought me so
much LAUGHter and
quiet thinking. BOOKS like
tHAt ARE Such Blessings
tRUtHFUL.-BRAVE.-RARE
I keep thinking ABOUt
WHEN I will Begin my
BOOK" AND that overwhelms me
Completely...THE truth is it has
Been written inside me and
IN THE RIGHt TIME MY BOOK WILL EMERGE to the WORLd.

I AM WATCHING THE CARS, BUSES, CABLE CARS and PEOPLE-ALL going UP and DOWN
EVERYONE IS ON THEIR WAY to A DESTINATION somewhere.
But it seems like THE "JOURNEY THERE" is really where the secret DETAILS ARE the things WE ARE to Be learning-THE corners AND EDGES OF OUR STORIES
EVERY MOMENT "ON THE WAY" is the destination.

READ: MOONLIGHT
THRONICLE

It feels hard to write.
I just don't want to.

                              but it's only the second day of this
                                new "MORNING WRITING " goal,
            I didn't sleep well last   night.
                              (I got the couch) it was really deep
                                                and i felt like
                                      I was sinking,
            I got all twisted up and now my back hurts, it was really windy
            and the shutters were banging.
                  and the worst part is that yesterday I tripped really badly.

ToDAY

I feel 15.   while running down the pathway to the beach with my sister
     and...   (she will make me admit that I was sort

1. dry   of going after a very cute boy
2. THICK   ) anyway...
3. chapped   I went flailing into the air with my high sandles
4. Lumpy   yes
                     I banged up the ball of my foot and
5. Beige   now it's blue and hurts.

SIX. WIDE   now I don't want to write.

7. Freckled   how is that for complaining?
   (extrA)   oh yes, and I also have aloe vera in my eye.
                                        ALOE
              this sounds like Alexander and the Terrible Horrible
                     no good day   by Judith Viorst
SOME DAYS ArE liKE tHis.   ↓VERY BAD.
                     and its's only 9am.

PANTS PANTS

$

GOOD?

I CAME HOME FROM a day AT the MALL WITH myself.
WHAT was I thinking? I THINK I WENT — to get away from my thinking

ROAMING WITH PLATFORM BOOTS
AND BLACK-suck in tummy PANts.
I WAS DRESSED TO BLEND into the mall

I'VE Been SEARCHING outward
not inward
I feel TIRED

my FEET ACHE
And I'VE GOT Red rubbed marks on my
anckles
WHERE THE ZIPPER
on my too HIGH BOOts
were scratching my legs as I
Legs
measuring myself
1 2 3 4 5 6 7 8 9
climbed up
and down the
ESCALATORS
Looking for
Outward
answers.

Sometimes I hate my body

MALL

IDEAL → unreal.
IDEAL

I TRIED ON TOO MANY JEANS.

Ideal Size

DUMB DAY

Boot cg
anc#le Fit
'slim fit'

I'll just
surrender to
Long skirts

THE Perfect Fit isn't the answer

C.P SHADE
is the best
Place FORe
Long skirts

Put on
what
you Love.

van morrison
overalls
A peach cobbler Break

MORE IS NOT ENOUGH

LUNCH at school

eating LUNCH at school

I'm in ONE of those compleatly
DISCONNECTED feels so crazy sort OF MOODS

I CAN FEEL
THAT MY HAIR is flat + wing-y on the sides

I really DO

Why does it matter so much here
so MUCH WATCHING
and FEELING
WATCHED.
—trying too hard—

sometimes I go to the Bathroom to look in the MIRROR just to make sure I'm still here

GET A GRIP
MY MIND CAN TAKE
ME SO FAR AWAY

soup.

Beet
Butternut
soup

awful awful awful awful

AM ALL ALONE

SEA

finding myself alone.

I MADE A COMFORT STATION IN MY LOCKER TO LOOK INTO WHEN I FEEL LOST FROM THIS WORLD.

Sometimes I want to go home.

it is FILLED WITH

1. Jasmine tea
2. EARL GREY TEA (HONEY PACKETS.)
two MUGS
angel cards   Honey

SOME SNACKS
GUM
RED LICORICE
ginger candy.
CHILDHOOD PICTURE
Present DAY family
PICTURE
ANNE Lamott
lavender LOTION
COMB.

grass is greener?
REMEMBER to
READ ✓

JOURNAL
OF A solitude
By May sarton
and
JENNY READ by Jenny Read

PABLO NERUDA
(THE BOOK OF QUESTIONS)

Sometimes

CRY

must. Be brave!
Grateful.

LING TO HOLD ONTO
I FEEL LIK

TIME. NEW TIME

CRY
FULL

eyes.

Protect + HOLD ON to...

WITHOUT COLOR

I try too much to protect what I wish I let BE FREE

my whole body was overcome with the ache of inadequacy

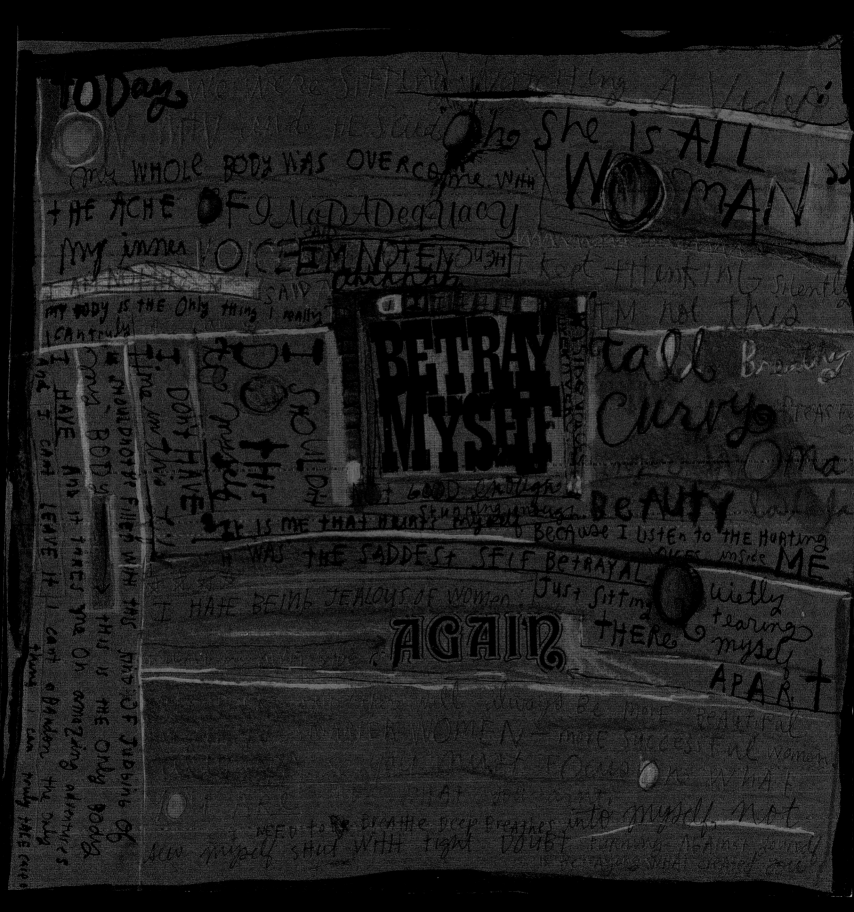

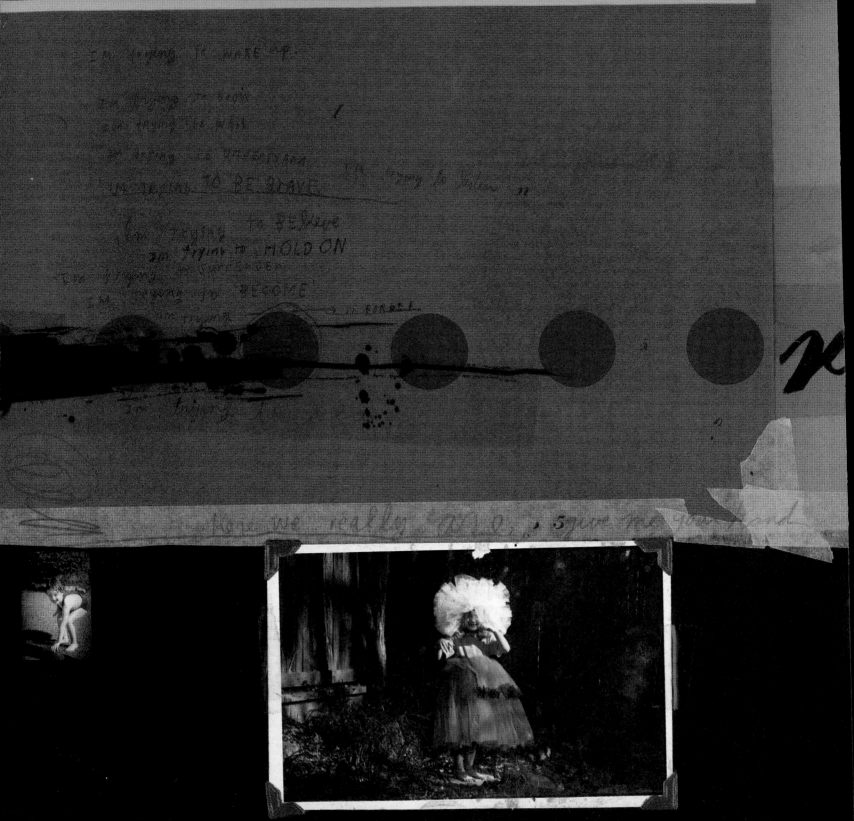

Sometimes I feel really terrible.
Sometimes I serge with power.
Sometimes I want to go home.

The BeST Way Out is is Always through.
                                    —R. frost

" If I had my life to live over   I'd try to make more
      mistakes next time. I would relax. I would Limber up.
I'd be sillier than I have been on this trip. I know of
a very few things I would take seriously.
    I would be less hygenic. I would take more ~~~~ chances
    I would take more trips.
I would climb more mountains, swim more rivers,
                     and watch more sunsets.
        I would burn more gasoline and eat more ice cream
                     and less beans.
    I would have actual troubles & fewer imaginary ones.
        you x see I'm one of those people who lives sensibly
        and sanely hour after hour, day after day.

                oh, I've had my moments,   *And If I had my LIFE to LIVE OVER I'd HAVE*
      in fact I'd have ~~nothing else just moments~~   ~~and if I had my~~ *MORE OF THEM*
                     ~~LIFE TO LIVE OVER I'd~~ have more of them. *In FACT*
                                                                  ~~but~~ Id
        just ————————→ moments one after another   *have*
                                                                nothing
                                                                else
                instead of living so many ~~~~ years ahead each day.
        I've been one of those people who never goes anywhere
      without a theremometer, hot water bottle, rain coat &
and parachute.

            If I had my life to live over I'd go places and do
THINGS AND TRAVEL LIGHTER THAN I have.
      ~~I would~~ If had my life to live over I would start
        Barefoot earlier in the spring & stay that way
        later in the fall. I would play hooky more.
    I wouldn't make such good grades, except by accident.
I'd ride more merry-go-rounds. I'd pick more dasies."

            NADINE STAIR age 85

                        Live

Tonight we drank porto Rico Sangria that Wilson brought home → WE sang to cherished songs on the old PIANO downstairs WE wore Flannel P.Js and sketchBookS Filled with the sea side. music Filled the NIGHT → FAVORITE songs TORi Amos TEAr IN Your HAIR CHINA WINTER.

This night reminds me of the First memories of living in THIS BIG Old Berkeley HOME.

I WOULD Lie On the oriental Rug IN Bare Feet and CLOSED EYES tears usually Rolled into my ears as Rebecca WOULD Sing + play THE PIANO

Rebecca is one of the SAFEST Humans I know → SHE IS LOVE the WITH HER I FEEL LIKE I CAN UNRAVEL and Be as BARE and "BLLAH" and euphoric and 'ACHY' and all the Rest. SHE Loves IN generous wide wonderful WAYS! SHE IS Also a Writer + actress like no other! THANK YOU Rebecca

We are here together AgAIN ToNIght. it seems to Be a tiny wrapped gift of A NIght For the two of us. TIMELESS and new AgAIN. FAMILIAR LAUGHTER

Rebecca And Me

5 6

6

what I LOVE

play

1 Sweet Potatos and cAmomile Tea

2 Long skirts

3 The color of old LEMONS

4 worn in pillow cAses

5 Pablo Neruda poetry

6 the Smell of FALL

7 grilled cheese

8 A clutched hand in the RAin

sandbars

12 fortune cookies

13

14 OAKtrees

15 BLUSHING

MoLLY → IN BETWEEN Two worlds searching.

Final ground.

On the phone

I HAD a pretty major talk with mom tonight
On the phone..

I HAVE FELT FRUSTRATED with our friendship.
KIND
I DON'T Like Calling HOME just for the "news".
I WANt to feel needed + connected +
~~valuable~~ VALUABLE. LATELY it HAS felt like AIR
Empty of the Real stuff.

I Am so glad we could talk about it. I think
WE cracked through the shell to the
realness of OUR FRIENDSHIP as Mother + DAUGHTER.

I came FROM HER → I want to
kNOW HER ~~truly~~.
TRULY.

Crimson
Honey,
COMB
CANDles
tONight

grow

NARCISSUS
~~Narcissus~~ BULBS
I Bought THREE

FIRST SUPERSONIC FLIGHT 194_

USA 32

Celebrating the Self

I HOLD tightly to
FRIGHTENED HANDS.
And kiss foreheads gently.

I know what
its like TOO feel
to deeply
and wander an
WONDER under
the LATE DAY
sun today
alone

READ Song of yourself | WALT WHITMAN

I tell my truth

I MAKE a lot
of mistakes
I tell my doubts
I LAUGH WITH my worries
I DANCE with little girls and I
WATCH SEA TURTLES
WITH NANA

I am frightened By TRUTH
sometimes → But I need it
LIKE MY OWN BLOOD

OPEN UP.

FINDING MY style AND not wearing Fitted BLACK PANTS.

IF I WAS to HAVE An Answer to this Growing PAin Question it would Be Something like THIS:

You've got this AMAZing Creature → YOURSELF.

THAT CAn move and Breathe, DAnCE and cry. And you have a certain amount OF MOMENTS (MAYBE a Few million moments — But And you HAVE THIS CHANCE to do absoloutly MOMEnts tHEY ArE) AnytHIng to rEACH OUT to AnotHEr vulnerable + TRUE. to dance on the roof in euphoniA AnD prAY BESiDE tHE OCEAN to LEt GO WE HAVE THE CHANCE every MOMENT to BE ALIVE and to GIVE to tHIS WOrld WHO nEEds EACH OnE of US So BADly

YELLOW BRICK ROAD

I know HOW TO LIE DOWN and stare at the sky and wonder about this life of mine.

[I know I love macaronni with ketchup

* I know How To slide my fingers along his neck and think about HOW much IT will ache at the end.

I know I am strong + soft and sore other times I KNOW I AM LOVED IN HUGE Deep Ways. I know I'm afraid of that to go away.

go to bed

00 a.m.

PREPARING

FOR WHAT "WILL HAPPEN Next,
and THE WORRies thAt go alone with it
getting READY FOR LIFE—not Being IN LIFE
it seems we stARt so young with the

get up **dress** **wash** **eat** **work** **undress** **bath**

[Routine]

NE "GROW UP" too fast.

If we stop there are so many
WORRIES OF WHAT could happen,
will be ~~fore~~ lose the connection?
WILL I BE "REPLACED"?
Will I BE forgotten?"

it IS EXHAUSTING—Gripping
onto too much!

I AM REMINDED OF MAY SARTON WRITING
IN JOURNAL OF A SOLITUDE

"IMMITATE THE TREES"
Let GO. cut off excess...prune
WAIT. WATCH. grow deep

WILL IT BE TAKEN AWAY?

REMEMBER THIS DAY.

AWAY A WAY

ALL
WAY

these day

I THINK GOD leave
me Alone to let
ME FIND MY OWN STRENGTH
BECAUSE no ONE else can give it TO ME
FOR ME
sometimes it is very lonely - but
the lonely times TEACH
ME the Most.

NO ONE CAN LOVE ME FOR ME.

take a Big Walk
in the
trees

BEFORE
I MISS THE time   today

Building FAITH — A talk with Chris... → knowing you survived. ☆ Book Dreams in New York
seeing PETER BEARD SHOW.

THE DIFFERENCE

BELIEVING → in SOMETHING 'KNOWN' - in our frame of reference

FAITH UNKNOWN
unseen

faith

How it really FEELS inside.

← megan.

AGE [19] PROJECT

↓

Being Open to things THAT COME outside Our frame of REFERENCE.

buttons

old tape

Pin (safety)

PAPER CLIPS

Little page ideas.

THE MOON SHEDS its SHADOW.

color proofs/
childhood image

THE JAPANESE hold MOON VIEWING PARTIES.

Thank you.

you know I love you but just can't take this anymore

BABY'S FIRST PLAYMATES:
THEIR NAMES AND WHERE THEY MET

deep Red

italic

blank   overflowing

— 1 . 1 4 2 . 0 5 4 0 5   3 . 9 2 . 1 4 0 5

USE loneliness Its ACHE

I bought first RED lipstick (really red) at BARNEYS

Draw

Life to you is a dashing and bold adventure.

REMBERING
LIFE

N°. 1 SHOES (SWING dancing)

2 eggs

3 plates Italian Dinners in the garden.

4 tops (TUBE tops + BOAT Necks)

5 tEA earl grey + cream

6 bathtubs under the MOON

7 grapefruit with honey

8 buttons c.p. holes

9. tomatos from daniel.

WATER   TEA

draw.

Make your own life.

nana

epiphanies.
alone

from LETTERS
to A Young poet BY: RAhier maria Rilke

Think, dear friend, reflect on the world
that you carry within yourself. And name this
thinking what you wish. It might be recollec-
tions of your childhood or yearning for your
own future. Just be sure that you observe care-
fully what wells up within you and place that
above everything that you notice around you.
Your innermost happening is worth all your
love. You must somehow work on that.

read

Iowa

F g H I

memories

Down The Center By Canoe

companions Solitude FEAR

I've BEEN AWAY FROM BERKELEY FOR A Week. It feel like
I DisappeareD From the WORLD — THAT WORLd — and come home
in Such A LARGER Sence OF The WorD. TOnight we maDe Berry piE
and ate ASPARAGUS WITH OuR fingers
(like Walt Whitman) WE WATCHED
tHE great MOVIE 'Beautiful DReamers'
under lots of QuiLts
I love this
funny family
 of mine

At _home_ (Last day of summer)
It is GOOD to sit HERE under
Huge knarled OAK trees in the late
AFTERNOON. It feels like life
HAS slowed down →to just look up at the
sky with MY DAD.

I   cl feel nearly only 8

HERE I Can Rest And Be AS
YOUNG AS I AM

* TAKE this feeling WITH ME.

I FEEL THE END OF THIS BOOK
arriving.

You know it is HAPPENING
when THE spine begins
and suddenly
the BOOK has
BECOME RIPE

WHAT a YEAR it has BEEN.
all these 1. QUESTIONS
2. Miracles
3. MUCK
4. CLARITY.
that have free from

→ simply trying
TO GROW
into MYSELF

(I think Growing Happens even when
Im not trying.

→ to creek

A full room

there has been

a lot of
TAKING in
And Letting
GO.
and GOODBYES.

→ MEGAN
/FAITH

→ First
PAinTING

your Freckles

WE SPEAK even when we
are no longer
speaking.

and oh how very you

I've been searching

A SHOW IDEA

I AM FINALLY HERE SITTING ALONE to
feel life - digest my
GROWING

AuntAnn is dying and I feel
REGRET that I didn't HEAR
all HER stORiES

her time PARIS in the 20's

I WISH I HAD ASked HER MORe QuestiOns
tell me tell me (we should
LIFE really is so short   always
                                 ask further)
WE HAVE SUCH LITTLE TIME
With eachother   listen. Bless.

o bravfeil
bottom

COME BACK TO ERIN

@ weeping Willow Today is
@ storm of rest Auntie ___
@ tiny wonder She offered ___
the OLD Photo ___
U wonder ___
Who you will one day find

I CANT see Her to say goodbye.
I feel like I HEAR HER
though

WHY IS it when we know someone is leaving
us → why is it then THAT WE CAN WHO
love them the DEEPEST? the closest TIME
IS WHEN WE SAY GOODBYE.
BEDTIME

love all the way
STAY
WHILE I CAN.

intricate
trying

2♥

Before we knew HOW to leave eachother

knowing someone else's life is passing away, makes me want to show up for LIVING now, not 'THEN' when 'things' are taken care of and the WEATHER IS WARM. TODAY I have a chance to make a diffrence NOW. I have a chance to HELP heal some of my OWN BROKEN places and hopefully someone elses

☆ WE MUST REALIZE THAT WHAT WE DO

Matters
our love matters truly
what remains long after I am gone
(THATS WHY WE ARE HERE)

Life is too short to be cruel, IT IS TOO SHORT to suck-in, HOLD IN, NOT FORGIVE WE JUST DONT Have time love is all there is to DO

FORGIVE YOURSELF

Signatures at various ages

Betty Bartman 7 yrs.
Betty Bartman 10 yrs.

Sabrina Ward Harrison

WE ARE
NOT SO different
only our
circumstances
are.

(take yourself
WITH YOU.)

I can't be here just to worry about the "Z" it or my chin, OK, the "seven" girls than me
OR MY BUTT- to- HIGH +ransition → and HOW
much I WANT HIM TO CALL.

I have to be here to do my PART to be Truly me. As Bravely As possible → with myself — with others. I must give what I know is TRUE
I must SHOW Up for my OWN life.
I must be REAL! again.
"I always noticing me.
"the WORLD wants to different
WHEN you remember to
Be original, not
imitate.

Don't turn against yourself
top
bottom
around
★ soul.

to. We are

WHOLE from
→ inner voice →

so here I am
today,
in the story
of
my life.

This is what I
know now.
These are my
questions
I ask.

mostly it's
tangled

but it's real.

and very little
seems
to be real anymore.

collect your

life.

treasure.

I am here alone for the first time in

weeks, to take up my "real" life again at last.

That is what is strange—that friends,
even passionate love, are not my real life

unless there is time alone in which to explore

and to discover what is happening or has happened.

MAY SARTON, JOURNAL OF A SOLITUDE

1. DOnt compromise yourself
free → FREE → yourself
StAY on your own Star
LIE DOWN under a
feel it the way through clear at night sky LISTEN
ALL
the weak
the strong
the real.
to → WHAT Falls silent behind your gaze.
And what

Growing up is like this. Living is like this
The Euphoria and the Ache, this
the Confusion and the Questions
the WONDERING, the understanding, the young and the Brave.
these Are the DAYs
tHat must HAPPEN
to ME. this I Believe.

BE *yourself* BE YOURSELF
contraDICTIONS EmBRACE them.
Own them.
Laugh with them.
I am Learning that.
WE ARE all of it.
the BASIC the AngRY the lonely the brave the true the lost the SCARED all of our edges
THERE isn't going to BE A point
of Completion (that is the hard part to realize)
IM not going to 'have' it all together'
Look @ How I "should Look"
feel How I "should feel" and.
DO what I "should BE doing"
because right Now is it Because right Now is it.
I don't know what will come next → How it will come.
I know. It neVER WORKS out How I think it WILL
looking BACK it always has worked out How
it SHOULD.

remember this   our
                        in life on on our own way

What I really want to say to myself is

IT is ALRight

THIS → right here this mess this
as my friend GAry says "IN its own
FlaWED WAy, It is all secretly perfect.

these anxious → Questions, DOUBts
Answers and waiting → this is just as
it is → right Now → taking me on my
ways → don't run. We all suffer

there will be This is What I know to Be
understanding
A → sooner than you think and later than you expected.

Sometimes IM just such A Mess.

Study? that voice inside that wispers YES

I have Learned

→ more is
never enough the World waits for
you.
~~We~~ Writing A BOOK Is Really
HARD:
and takes a really long time.
and a Hell of alot of FAITH
writing is mostly about letting go and loosening
the muscles of the heart

I am learning that growing is a mixture
Of Surrendering to that none of it ~~matters~~
And All of it Matters

the DeTAils of our lives and
our truth it is about → WHAT WE STAND
UP FOR → and what
WE Let go Of. this is the
real stuff

Accepting myself Brings me

AWAY FROM ANALYZING

DOUBTING Comparing

ALTERING HOW I AM.

WHO I AM

It GIVES ME SPACE to DANCE
and BE BAREFOOT and ForGIVE and
Write BrAVELY even WHEN it Feels Scary and

AWKWARD, it is WHO I AM
it is important TO SHARE and

NECESSARY to Live.

As TANGLED and TRUE as it is.

I AM realizing that I am enough as is → a WORK IN PROGRESS

I HAVE looked at the love that surrounds me... the new LOVE and HIDDEN LOVE, and DESIRED LOVE. BUT SOMETHING changes when I SLOWLY turn my LOVE TOWARDS myself

tHats when my LIFE BEcomes VIVIDLY FULL color. I think in healing ourselves WE can take PART in healing tHE WORLD

I CAN see the Life in me,

I CAn stop HIDINg my FRECKLES

I CAN Look deeply into my own eyes, And high up into tHE Branches of trees, I can BEcome myself...

SABrina

MARIA

REPRint permissions

1. Journal of A SOLITUDE ——→ By May Sarton. copyright © 1973
by May SARTON. Reprinted by permission of W.W. Norton & company, INC.

2. Letters to A Young Poet by RAiner Maria Rilke.
copyright © 1992 by New WORLD Library.
reprinted by Permission by New World Library

3. ——→ EVERY girl Is a Princess, an unpublished POEM
by Meagan De Wolf. Reprinted by permission
Of Meagan MEAGAN De Wolf and Kathryn Shepler.

4. EVery effort Has been Made to contact all rights
holders of the material in Spilling Open. The author
promises to correct any omissions or mistakes in
future editions.

1
THREE
2
5
SIX
7
8
9
10

DAN MEL BRI + SAB
Summer 1994

Photography & ART Permissions are on this PAGE.

→ 1. Photographs of Sabrina Ward Harrison. Permission granted by photographer

2. Photograph of Sabrina. Permission granted by Photographer AMANDA Marsalis!

3. Photograph of Kathleen H. MORFORD taken by Sabrina Harrison Tymarel COOK
permission bRANTED by kathleen morford.

4. PHOTOGRAPH of Marguerite Monosoff-RICHARDS, taken By Jamie Pillers. Permission GRANTED By JAMIE Pillers and Cynthia RICHARDs + Mari RICHARDS

5. PHOTOGRAPH Photographs of Elise Kohl-Grant, taken by Sabrina Harrison PERMISSION bRANTED By Elise Kohl-bRANT and Bill bRANt.

6. PHotographs of Raymond Kohl-Grant taken by Sabrina Harrison. permission granted By Raymond Kohl-Grant and BiLL GRANt

7. PHotograph of Mia Rae Benenate, By Sabrina Harrison. Permission granted by Mia Benenate + Becky Benenate

8. PHotographs of Nicole Sherman and Lilli Sherman taken By Sabrina Harrison. Permission granted By Lilli Sherman, Nicole Sherman + Laura Duldner

9. Art contributed BY MEAGAN De WOLF. Permission granted By meagan DeWolf and Kathryn Shepler

10. ARTWORK entitled Believe By Alexander R. Kopps in collaboration with Sabrina W. Harrison. Permission granted By Alexander KOPPS.

11. Photograph of Hannah Finnie By Sabrina Harrison. Permission granted By Hannah Finnie and penelope Finnie.

12. all the childhood pictures of me taken by JOHN + LOIS HARRISON.

THANK YOU All

a time to be born and a time to die, a time to plant and a time time to heal, a time to build, a time me to mourn and scatter stones

orn and a time to uproot, a time ime to tear down to weep and a time a time to dance AND a time to g

o die, a time to e to kill and a n and a time to to laugh, a ti~ e, a time to ather them,

a time to embrace and a time time to search and a time to to keep and a time to throw tear and a time to mend silent and a time to spea

to refrain, a give up, a time away, a time to a time to be k, a time to

love and A for WAR There is a and A sea under.....

time to hate and a time time for EV son for every HEAVEN.

A time for PEACE. ERything, activity

ECCLESIASTES 3:1-8